# When Spring Comes

## ROBERT MAASS

HENRY HOLT AND COMPANY · NEW YORK

For Hillary

Henry Holt and Company, Inc., *Publishers since 1866*
115 West 18th Street, New York, New York 10011

Henry Holt is a registered trademark of Henry Holt and Company, Inc.

Published in Canada by Fitzhenry & Whiteside Ltd.,
195 Allstate Parkway, Markham, Ontario L3R 4T8.

Library of Congress Cataloging-in-Publication Data
Maass, Robert.
    When spring comes / Robert Maass.
    1. Spring—Pictorial works—Juvenile literature.   [1. Spring.]   I. Title.
    QB637.5.M3   1993      508—dc20       93-29816

ISBN 0-8050-2085-3 (hardcover)
10  9  8  7  6  5  4  3  2  1
ISBN 0-8050-4705-0 (paperback)
10  9  8  7  6  5  4  3  2  1

First published in hardcover in 1994 by Henry Holt and Company, Inc.
First Owlet paperback edition, 1996
Printed in the United States of America on acid-free paper.∞

Spirits soar when spring comes.

A sweet fresh breeze blows.
Bright shades of green
decorate winter's bare trees.

Farmers plow or burn off
last year's stubble to get
the earth ready for planting.
Spring is the time to sow seeds
so there'll be crops
later in the year.

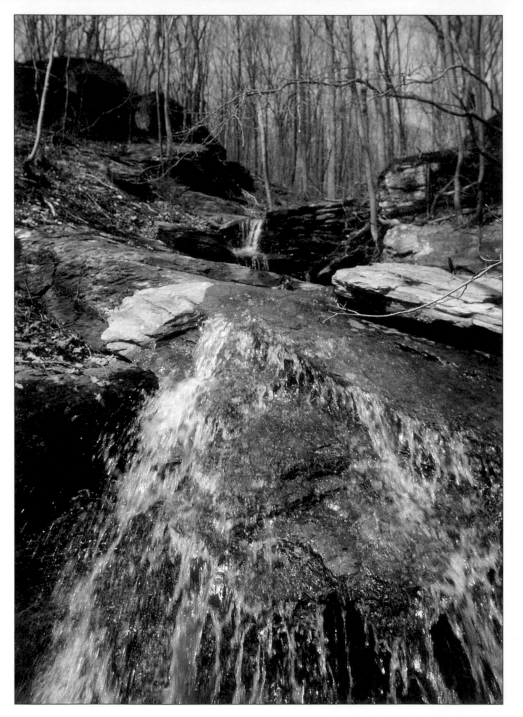

Rain and melting snow
make spring waters rush.
The season's warm days
and cool nights mean
maple sap can rise and
be tapped.

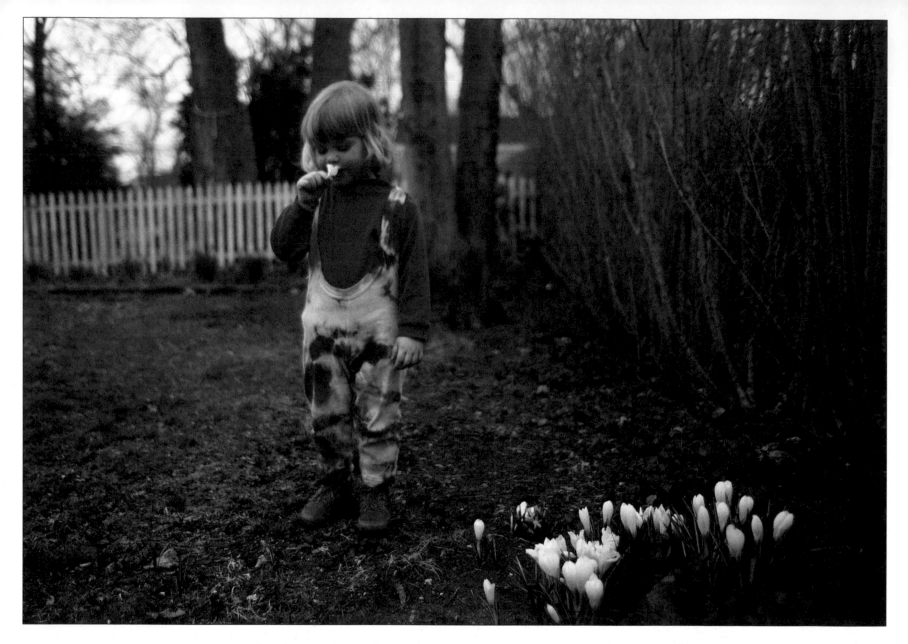

Crocuses peek their heads above the ground when spring comes.

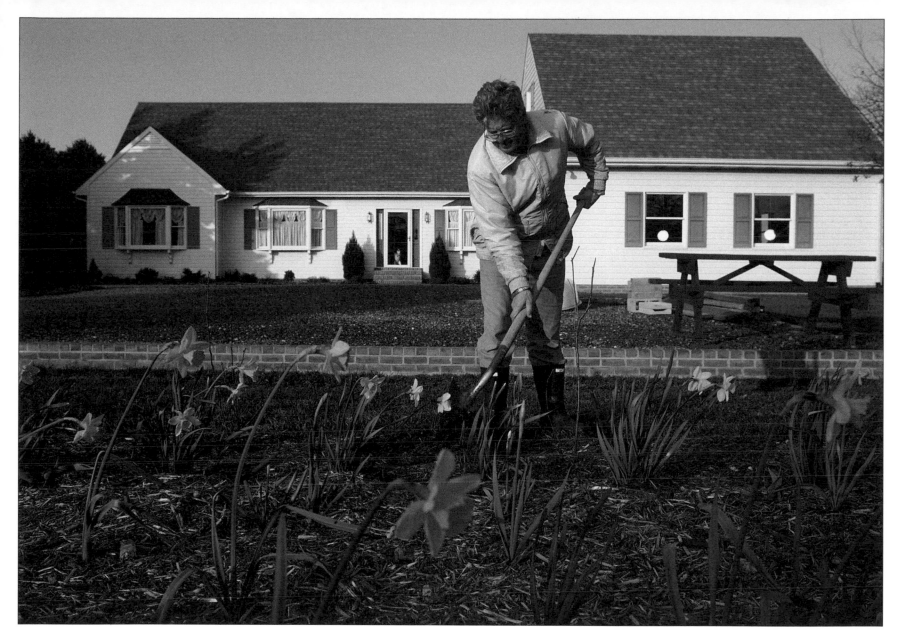

Gardeners turn the soil so last year's bulbs will return to flower.

Animals big and small are born in springtime.
Foals nuzzle their dams.

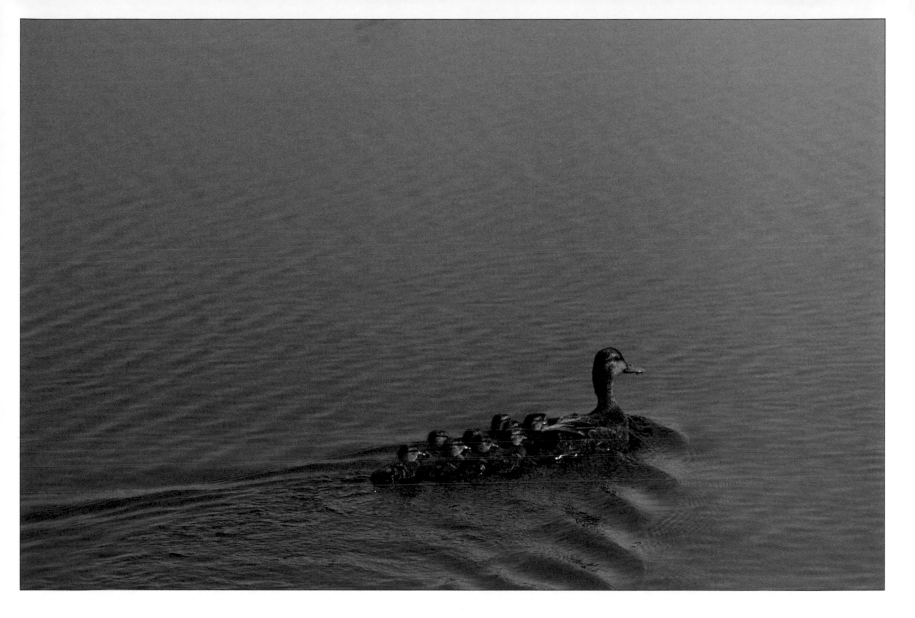

A mother duck seems to say "make way for ducklings!"

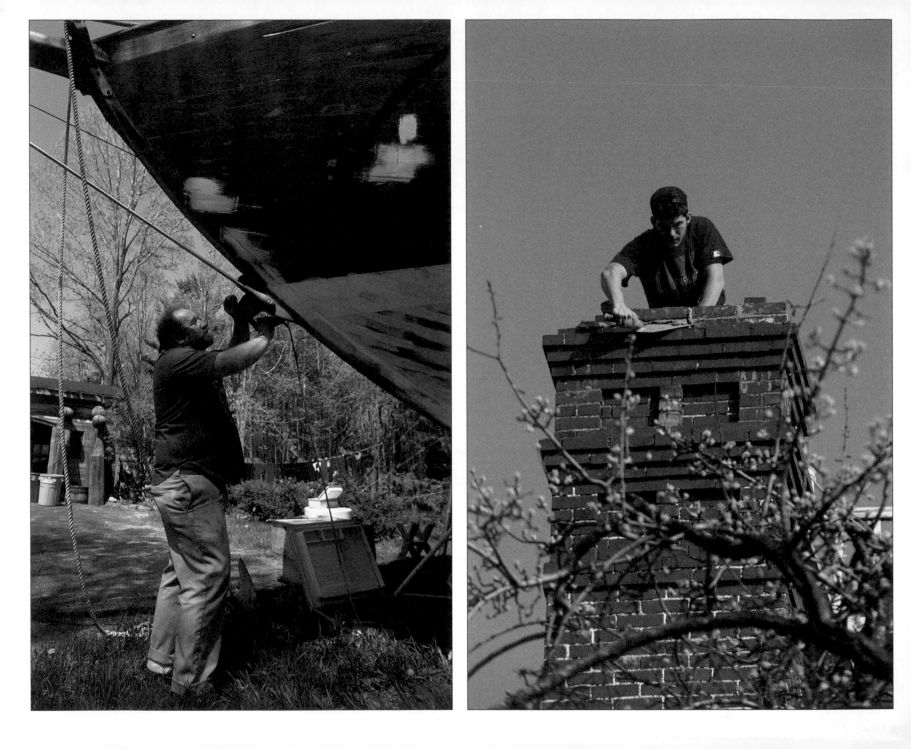

After the long winter,
boats need sanding,
brick needs pointing,
and roofs need mending.

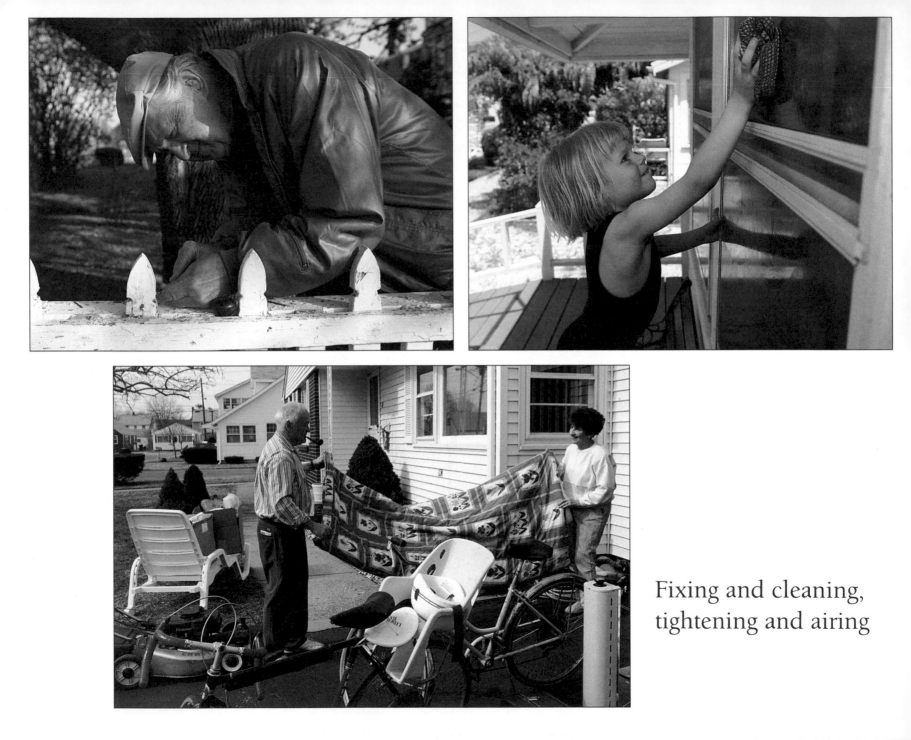

Fixing and cleaning,
tightening and airing

are spring tasks of repair and renewal.

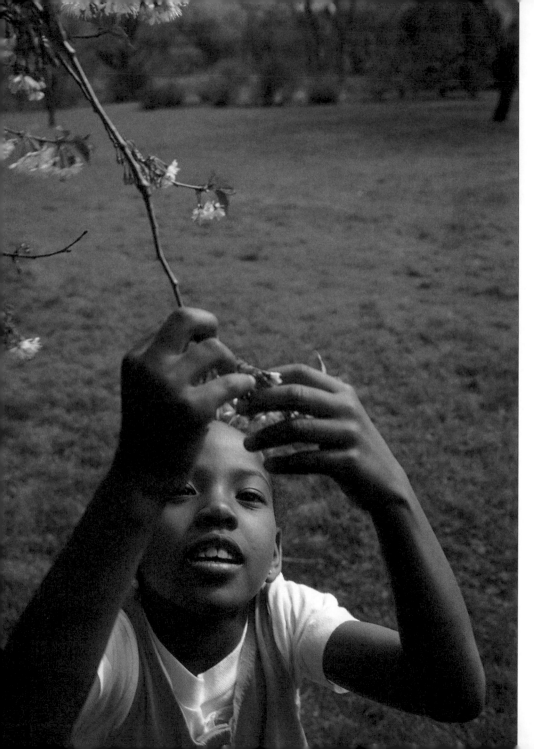

When all the world turns
green and flowery again,

a blossom is enough
to inspire a painting.

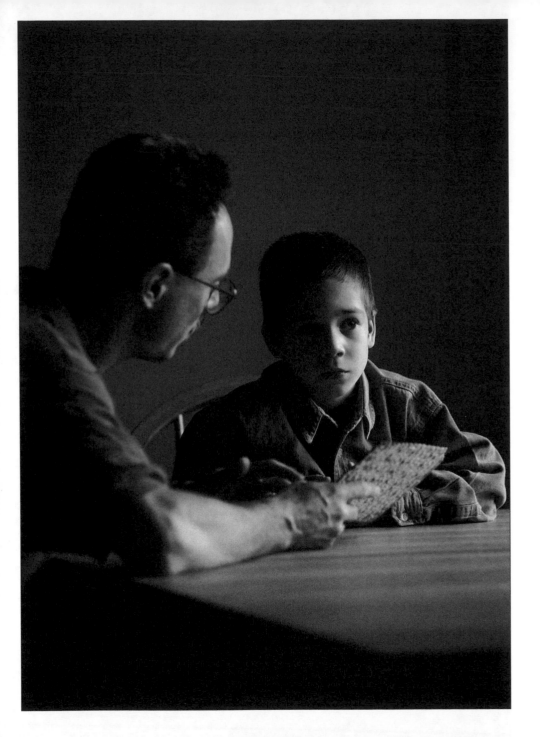

Matzoh is part of
every Passover seder,
when families gather to
retell an ancient story.

Bonnets and bunnies
appear at Easter.
It's time
to hunt for eggs.

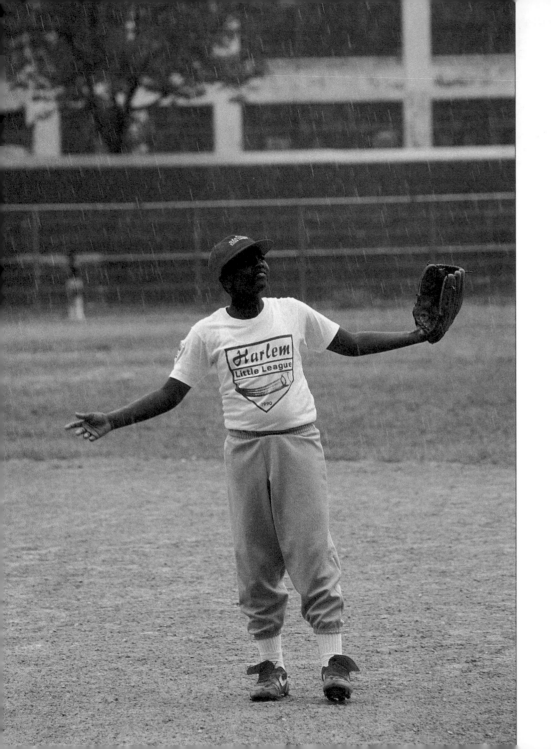

April showers
bring rain delays…

and May flowers.

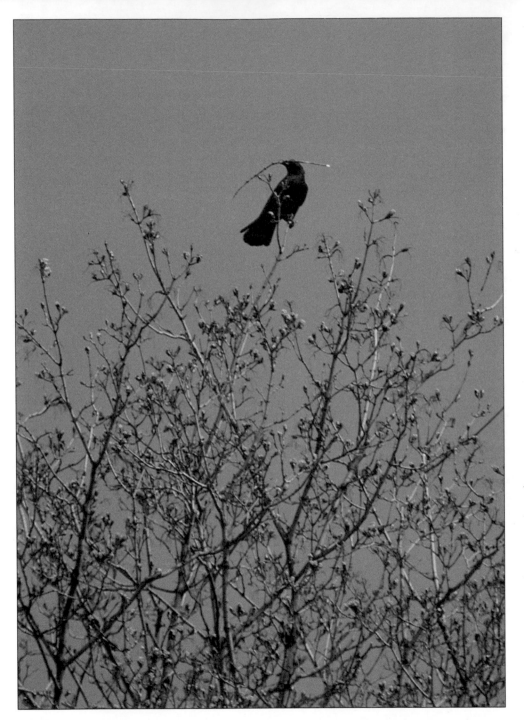

When spring comes,
birds return from
winter homes and busily
build their nests
(as people curiously look on).

On May Day, there's dancing and Maypoles, music and sunshine.

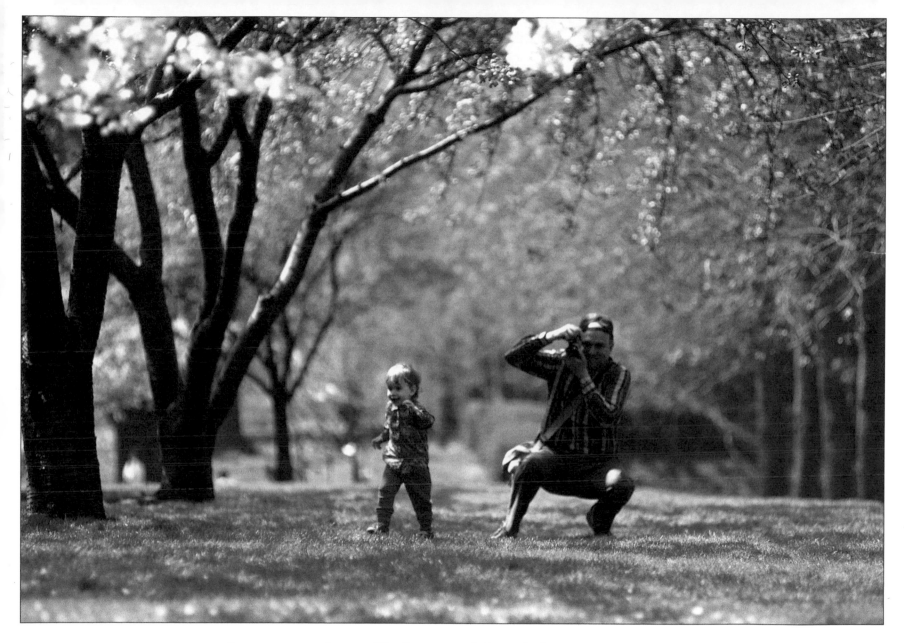

It seems that all the world celebrates spring.

Tradition has it that spring is a time for love to blossom

and be affirmed.

As the season nears its end, and hot weather approaches,

we mark Memorial Day
to honor those who've fallen
for their country.

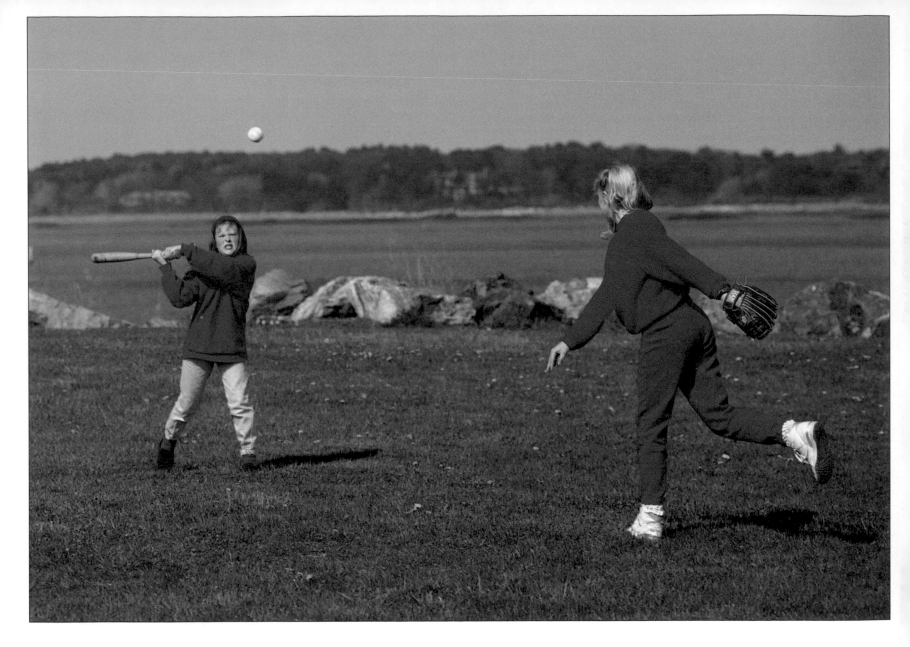

Spring makes us ready for the seasons to come. Roll on, summer!